I0815359

DIRTY ANIMAL JOBS

Kenny Abdo

Fly!
An Imprint of Abdo Zoom
abdobooks.com

abdobooks.com

Published by Abdo Zoom, a division of ABDO, P.O. Box 398166, Minneapolis, Minnesota 55439.

Printed in the United States of America, North Mankato, Minnesota.
052025
092025

Photo Credits: AdobeStock, Alamy, AP Images, Getty Images, Shutterstock
Production Contributors: Kenny Abdo, Jennie Forsberg, Grace Hansen
Design Contributors: Candice Keimig, Neil Klinepier, Colleen McLaren

Library of Congress Control Number: 2024947692

Publisher's Cataloging-in-Publication Data

Names: Abdo, Kenny, author.
Title: Dirty animal jobs / by Kenny Abdo
Description: Minneapolis, Minnesota : Abdo Zoom, 2026 | Series: Dirty work | Includes online resources and index.
Identifiers: ISBN 9781098288693 (lib. bdg.) | ISBN 9781098289393 (ebook) | ISBN 9781098289744 (Read-to-me ebook)
Subjects: LCSH: Sanitation--Juvenile literature. | Careers--Juvenile literature. | Wildlife--Juvenile literature. | Animal husbandry--Juvenile literature. | Animal waste--Juvenile literature.
Classification: DDC 331.70--dc23

TABLE OF CONTENTS

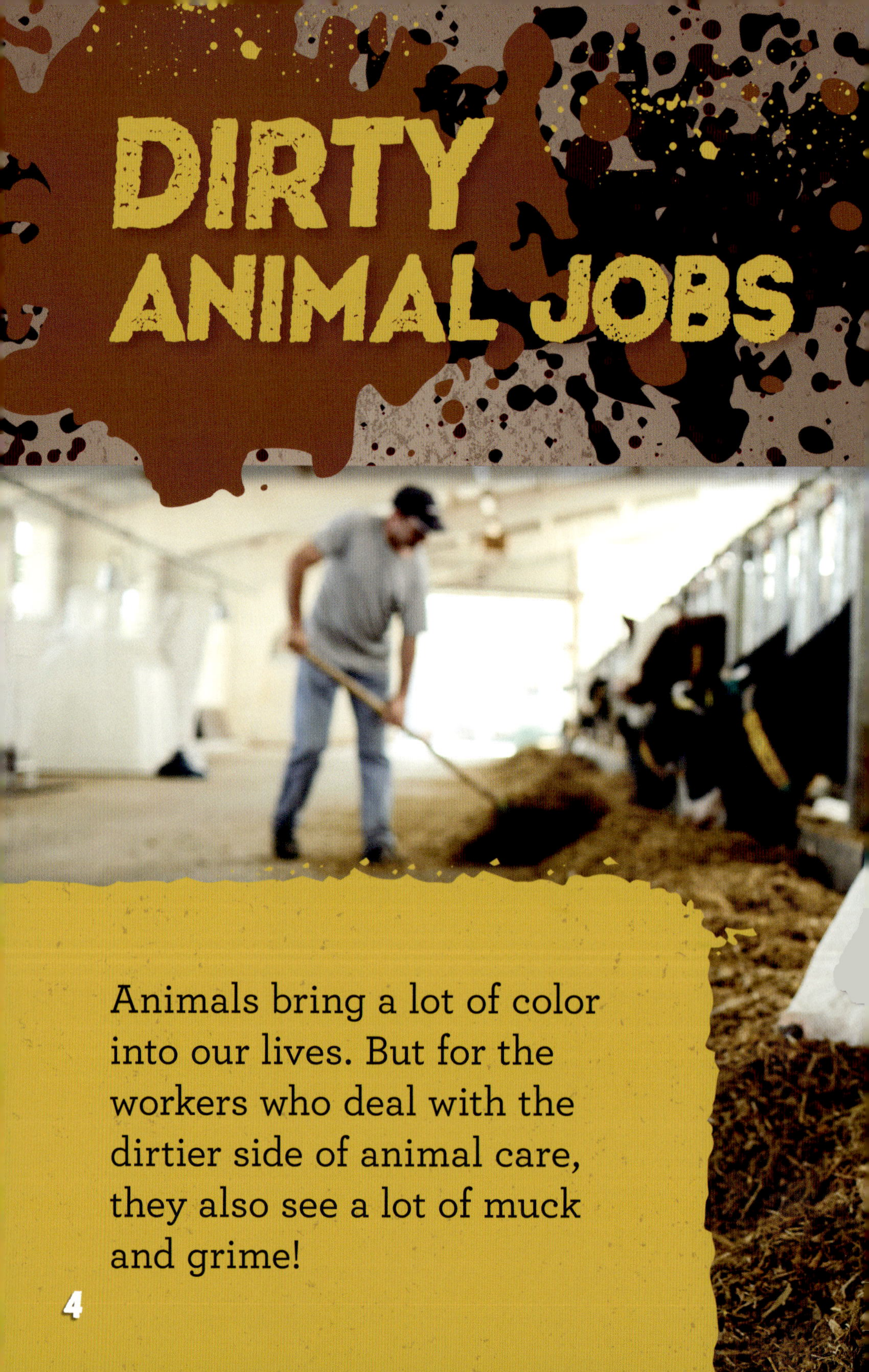

DIRTY ANIMAL JOBS

Animals bring a lot of color into our lives. But for the workers who deal with the dirtier side of animal care, they also see a lot of muck and grime!

NL 6667
0702

THE DIRT

Pet care workers are very important. They make sure animals are happy, healthy, safe, and clean!

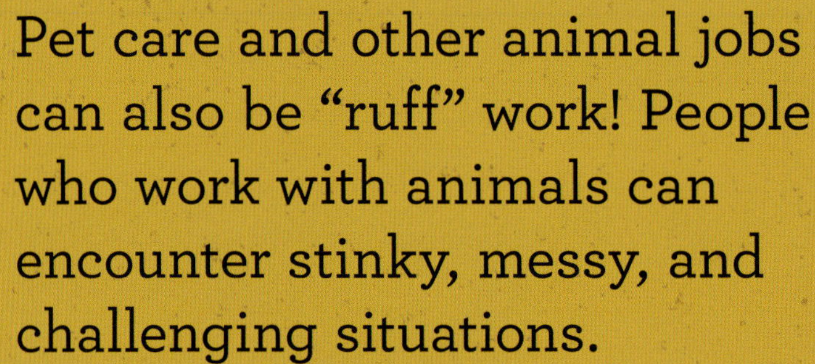

Pet care and other animal jobs can also be "ruff" work! People who work with animals can encounter stinky, messy, and challenging situations.

THE WORK

Pest control workers rid businesses and homes of mice, bugs, and other creepy crawly pests. Workers must first find how the pests are getting in and take care of the problem, no matter how gross!

Pet food companies want to make sure their product is the best it can be. They have people, called pet food tasters, try the pet food. Don't worry, though! They take small bites and then spit it out.

Taxidermists help those who have had a pet pass away keep their memory alive. They prepare the animal's skin so they can shape the body to create realistic displays. Taxidermists also create hunting trophies and museum **exhibits**. While it is hard work, they can make any animal **lifelike** in a stitch!

What pooper scoopers do is in the name. They pick up dog poop from public parks and private yards. Scoopers work in all kinds of weather to make sure the places pets play are clean. It is a job that you would not want two scoops of!

THE HOME DEPOT
HOMER
PAINT
BUCKET

Pet detectives roam the streets searching for lost pets. They look in all sorts of places, like under porches or even in trash cans. Sometimes, they find the animals safe. Other times, the mystery remains unsolved.

Fish processors prepare caught fish to be sold and eaten. They cut and clean the fish while working in cold and wet conditions. Dealing with strong smells and slimy insides, this is a seafood you don't want to see!

The life of a pet **influencer** manager can get pretty messy. Managers make sure pets look great for photos and videos. They also clean up messes and deal with animals that can be real **divas**!

Slaughterhouse workers help prepare animals to be turned into food. They must handle things like blood and animal parts. While slaughterhouse conditions can be gross, the work is a cut above the rest.

THE CLEAN UP

Some animal care workers shed the dirt from the job. **Conservation** officers protect nature and wild animals. They work hard to keep many animal **species** from disappearing forever. In 2020, they helped save more than 40 kinds of birds and mammals!

Dirty animal jobs play a critical role in helping animals live happy, healthy lives. While scooping poop or testing pet food may seem unpleasant, they are *pawsitively* essential for the well-being of animals!

GLOSSARY

conservation – the act of protecting and managing natural environments so plants and animals can live healthily.

diva – someone who is self-important and difficult to please.

exhibit – something that is shown or displayed for people to look at, like art in a museum.

influencer – an influential person in social media networks, often with a large following, who promotes the products and services of a brand.

lifelike – something that looks or acts like it was alive.

pest – an insect or animal that causes damage or is harmful in other ways.

species – a group of living things that look alike and can have young together.

ONLINE RESOURCES

Booklinks
NONFICTION NETWORK
FREE! ONLINE NONFICTION RESOURCES

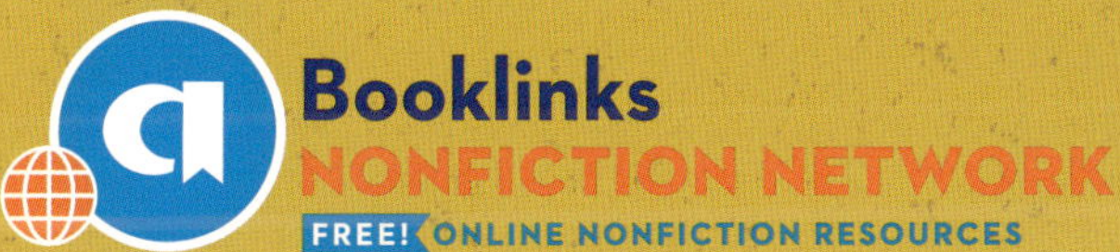

To learn more about dirty animal jobs, please visit abdobooklinks.com or scan this QR code. These links are routinely monitored and updated to provide the most current information available.

INDEX